M000191034

Table of Contents

○
○○○○
○○○○○○○
○○○○○○○○○○○
○○○○○○○○○○○○○○○
○○○○○○○○○○○○○○○○○○
○○○○○○○○○○○○○○○○○○○○○
○○○○○○○○○○○○○○○○○○○○○○○○
○○○○○○○○○○○○○○○○○○○○○○○○○○○
○○○○○○○○○○○○○○○○○○○○○○○○○○○○○
○○○○○○○○○○○○○○○○○○○○○○○○○○○○
○○○○○○○○○○○○○○○○○○○○○○○○○
○○○○○○○○○○○○○○○○○○○○○○
○○○○○○○○○○○○○○○○○○
○○○○○○○○○○○○○○○
○○○○○○○○○○○
○○○○○○○
○○○○
○

Dedication:

Community

Original Intuitive Writings

Give Her What She Wants

Who are you to deny giving One who makes your Heart sing
anything?

Do we not live in an infinite Universe in which all is provided for?
Do you want to live in a state of joy and abundance?
Then give Her what She wants.
And give it with joy.

Isn't giving, the same as receiving?
Then give Her what She wants by saying. "Yes, it's my pleasure."
This opens the back of the heart allowing you to receive more than
you can imagine.

If She was out late, celebrate Her fun with Her.
If She falls in love, celebrate the new love with Her.
What She wants is to feel safe in Her expression.
What She wants is for you to listen to Her.
What She wants is for you to feel Her.
What She wants is to feel alive.

She won't rest however, until you learn to listen from the innocence of your Heart.

If She wants freedoms, give them to Her.
If She wants her own space, give it to Her.
If She wants money from you, give it to Her.
If She wants a release from you, grant Her wish.

All you can do is give Her what you are ready to receive for yourself.

But, what if She wants to fight?

Then give Her something She cannot fight against.
Invite Her beyond the madness.

Allow Her to explore all desires.
Desires of the Heart manifest great things.
Desires of the shadow won't, but they do guide a person into their truth.
And this is what scares you.
From this point give Her what She <u>really</u> wants - which is Love.

Love Her problem.

Love Her struggle.

Love Her craziness.

Love Her addiction.

Love Her challenge.

If you give Her a fight, you are the one who is fighting.

If you are fixing a problem you see in Her, you are the problem yourself.

If you resist, you become the resistance.

Let Her go into the journey of Her insecurities and Her desires while you feel deeply from innocence.

When She feels safe in Her expression, your twin Hearts allow an initiation of purification.

The old painful patterns and stories are swept up and burned away in your sacred union.

Now you have given Her what She really wants.

A Woman, in Her fullest creative expression is a Goddess who can manifest anything She sets Her mind and Heart upon — and does so without condition. Her gifts emerge and are highly valued.

She is always safe and provided for, and the community around Her is elevated.

Which is why what you are wanting is irrelevant.

What purpose do you serve by trying to get sex, or an agreement, or attention from Her, when you can receive so much more?

Look at Mother Earth.

When you give Her what She wants, how does She respond?

When you fulfill your own desires first, what happens to the Earth?

Then Give Her What She Wants... She's The Momma.

<u>O</u>rigin

0000

$0+0+0+0 = \underline{O}$

○

Origin

Walking alone amongst a few thousand people at a music festival, I bump into an acquaintance – a man who I know is in the throws of a difficult divorce.

He explains how he is fighting his soon to be ex-wife for custody of his three young children.

"What do you want?" I ask him.

"I want the kids, and She won't let me have them. So I have hired a lawyer and I'm going after Her with everything I have."

His sternness amuses me. He is seemingly ignorant of the joy, laughter, music and song surrounding us.

"How is your business? Are you happy? Are things flowing well?" I ask.

The answer to each of my questions is somber.

"What does **She** want, I inquire?"

"She wants the kids – full time," he responds.

"Would you like to prosper, enjoy your children *and* be happy?" I ask.

"Of course," he replies.

I hear myself say:

"*Then Give Her What She Wants… She's The Momma.*"

There was my reflection, right in my face.

Hearing myself say these words: *Give Her What She Wants,* gave me a new curiosity about my own perceived shortcomings in relationship.

I could see how my friend's desire for self-preservation had caused him to take a combative stance, but also how fighting Her desire would create suffering for his entire family.

Was this a malicious posture, human conditioning, or something else?

I set the intent to find the truth of my relationship to these words.

Shortly thereafter, a series of intuitive writings entitled *Give Her What She Wants* provided me with an evolved way of communication. I became astonished how the nature of my reality quickly shifted, simply by using this evolved language.

I felt increased joy and experienced more meaningful relationships. My life purpose became clear and expressive. A vibrant community sprung up around me, and my creativity expanded.

Meanwhile, a new vision of human potentiality revealed itself.

Most impactful however, was this new ability to hear the wisdom in the voices of the women around me. It was like discovering a new code granting me access to a field of linguistic intelligence.

Linguistic Intelligence?

Yes.

Traditional language is built on the three elements of <u>word</u>, <u>tone</u> and <u>gesture</u>, which are a direct reflection of a dominant Holy Trinity in the civilized world – Father, Son, Spirit – a distinctly masculine orientation.

These three language elements connect together as sub-atomic particles becoming the essence of the sound waves of intelligence formulating the collective reality.

Because there are three elements, these invisible linguistic building blocks connect together triangularly.

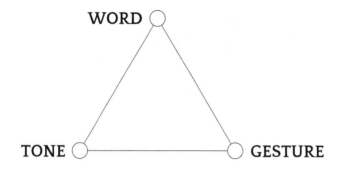

This language has been essential for self-preservation, much like the arrowhead. Its masculinity has allowed humans to survive, build and create structure. It has effectively brought us to this moment in our history.

Paradoxically like the arrowhead, language can be fashioned into sharp points creating division and limiting potential. Its structure allows for conflict, criticism, competition, and control. It is the language of inequality and condition: winners and losers, us and them, rich and poor, Heaven and Hell, and survival of the fittest.

Language allows us to shame, and be shamed.

By simply adding a fourth element to language, we have the power to soften its sharpness and eliminate its divisiveness, thereby activating an evolved Heart Language for human sovereignty.

Adding the element of <u>compassion</u> to the three elements of <u>word</u>, <u>tone</u> and <u>gesture</u>, changes the base sub-atomic structure of language.

Compassion is distinctly feminine.

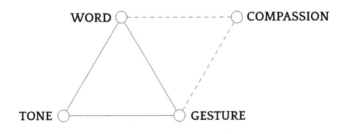

By opening the Heart as the initiation point of communication, we honor the Feminine gifts of nurture, nature and creativity. It is this honoring of compassion which opens a new door of awareness for humanity.

We literally stretch language into a new arrangement of empowerment using compassionate communication. By speaking and listening from the Heart with feeling, the way we communicate becomes (w)holistic – as both the masculine and Feminine energies are honored and balanced as One.

These building blocks of language suddenly become pyramid-shaped. The structure of this evolved language gives us access to the new empty space inside the expanded pyramid structure.

Inside this empty space is Divine Love consciousness.

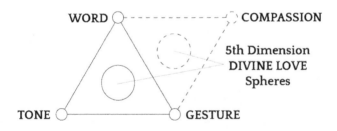

In Divine Love, the base sub-atomic building elements are holographic spheres.

These holographic spheres are available to organize our three-dimensional reality into perfect collaborative unity. It is an ever-present invisible holographic structure supporting an evolutionary leap for humanity.

These spheres are self-organizing, patterning themselves in harmony with the vibration of Linguistic Intelligence, giving humanity an evolved way of creating a reality of human sovereignty by aligning intent, compassionate language and inspired action with Divine Love.

With Heart Language, we honor our Self and all people with compassion. It is this honoring of what is inherent and natural to human beings, that allows us access to a higher level of intelligence.

From this higher level of intelligence we enjoy an expanded awareness to immediately see and act upon the solutions to our current challenges.

We become:

- Open to life, inside and out.
- Emergent from surviving to thriving.
- Completely transformational instead of competitively relational.

We naturally shift from hoping things will work out, to experiencing life happening better than we could have ever planned. We easefully leap from wanting things to be a certain way, to enjoying life the way it is. We evolve from masculine division and competition into a new spirit of Feminine collaboration. We begin to enjoy safety and well being on all levels.

Here, there are no conditions to receiving, so we all get what we all need.

Drawn to others speaking the Heart Language, groups of people are naturally formulated who no longer hear nor react to the divisive language of the collective, and are inspired to connect and create together what humanity has not yet been able to build:

A planet where everyone gets what they want.

Giving Her What She Wants is the initiation step to join a growing human sovereign movement. Saying yes to Her recognizes something so inherent in all human hearts, and yet is hidden away in the collective: True abundance is measured by the appreciation of the gift rather than the amount of personal gain.

At the Heart of this sovereign human movement is an invitation from Her - to all of us:

Honor Human Intimacy

In the Fall of 2014, I opened my heart to a circle of Women, ages 8-60, requesting they hold a sacred container of collective intent for this book to play an instrumental role in the evolution of human consciousness. I am deeply grateful for their participation, and incredibly appreciative for the creative alchemy initiated. The wisdom I continue to receive is astonishing to me.

Give Her What She Wants offers a modality of relationship that empowers men to become genuinely receptive and women to become authentically expressive.

Receptive men and expressive women who explore the empty spaces of Linguistic Intelligence, naturally balance the feminine and masculine energies, allowing a Heart Presence to emerge.

The Heart Presence is a feeling of radical trust, which empowers men and women to step fully into their respective gifts in service to humanity, together.

In Heart Presence, a woman feels safe enough to fully express Her sacred creative power – to embody a Goddess and sing the song of Her Heart.

It is when She feels She can be compassionately heard without conflict, competition, or control, Her Heart opens and the wisdom of Divine Love flows through Her.

Heart Presence guides Her to Her purpose: To bring balance and health to everything and everyone around Her.

A man in Heart Presence with a Goddess softens: He is no longer critical, striving for success, trying to fix problems, or exercising control over Her or in the world. The man is simply being present because he recognizes the power of connected Hearts in Divine Love initiates more valuable projects than he can start by himself or with other men.

Heart Presence guides him to His purpose: to serve the Feminine in providing for the community by ways of nature, nurture and creativity.

Heart Presence then, becomes the new currency of the Feminine Age, giving birth to an evolved lifestyle, arising from the feminine leadership inherent in women *and* men.

Feminine Leadership is the human emergence of the next Holy Trinity: Masculine, Feminine, and Heart, where Men and Women are individually empowered and unified in purpose.

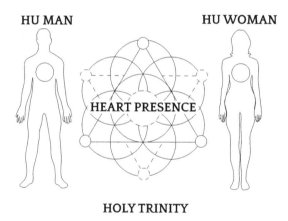

In this book, I share from my human perspective the emergence of the Feminine Leadership in me as a paradoxical offering: To utilize my experiential storytelling as an opportunity for all of us to evolve beyond the stories we believe about the human experience to open to something uncomfortable yet essential for our evolution.

It is time to face one another and take off our masks to reveal our truths for healing and transformation.

Therein lies the intent for this book: To Heal, and it starts with me.

Join me on a journey of a simple story that includes my intuitive writings, but most importantly the words of wisdom spoken by the women during the creation of this text.

The story is set in Mexico, Christmas 2013; and in linear time transpires a few hours, and then skips into the Now.

Its purpose is merely to give us a narrative to explore the opening of a new dimension of consciousness, making compassionate people the co-creators of a new reality of earthly playfulness.

Now.

From the Heart,

For Human Illumination.

A Book about Linguistic Intelligence.

Language is the quickest way to change consciousness.

See Goddess

1111

$1+1+1+1=4$

See Goddess

It is one of those beautiful days just before Christmas in Mexico. The beach is filled with locals and tourists. My heart is open and I am relaxed. There is a slight breeze, a few clouds. It's 83 degrees and perfectly perfect.

There are people everywhere. Vendors, musicians, teenagers, college students and families. The atmosphere is festival-like, without a discernable focus, except for the surfers and the waves. I feel the collective sigh of relief from time away from "the real world." Laughter, happy chatter and the smells of food cooking permeate the senses.

My daughters have been with me for a few days and while I have been feeling the potentiality of being challenged by having two teenagers on the beach as a single father, only in this moment does the reality of the challenge present itself.

Their Mother is back in the States, and this is my first time out of the country with the children since the divorce.

My eldest daughter is 17. She is a stunning woman on a journey of empowerment. She has a gift with a hula-hoop.

People are ten rows deep on the beach… and we have chosen to set up our camp in the midst of the chaos, and are soon to be center stage.

It's a gold hula. She is wearing a colorful bikini. Everything seems to be sparkling. Her strawberry ginger hair blows in the wind as She takes the hoop from its resting place in the sand and begins to warm up.

For most of my life, I have been bothered by other fathers speaking of 'protecting' their daughters by using intimidation on the young suitors who come on date night.

It was my inner dissatisfaction with how culture treats women, which led me to believe I always wanted sons. I imagined I could educate boys in a way that would affect the women in their relationships. This stayed with me until the moment my eldest surprisingly emerged from the womb with a vagina, and in that moment I felt the beginnings of the grace of raising a girl, then two and now three.

Years later, I socially reconnect with a friend who at 40, has become pregnant. She is thrilled to share the news of becoming a mother by patting Her belly and saying, "I'm having a boy!"

"But you know," She says, looking me in the eyes and raising Her voice for effect, "I only have to be concerned about his one penis, where as you have to be concerned with the thousands of penises which will come for your girls."

There are several women standing with us, and everyone has a good laugh. But, there is an undeniable truth of Her words that rock me. Yes, many men would come into contact with my daughters over their lifetimes.

As I have watched my older daughters come of age, I have quietly celebrated their emerging sexuality. Somehow, I have known that having any resistance to their emergence only keeps them and me from empowerment.

And yet, it's a jungle out there. And, it's certainly a jungle here on the beach. There is nothing but skin as far as the eye can see.

Just behind me, my attention shifts to a family of three getting into an argument. I cannot hear everything they are saying, but the father is refusing his teenage daughter something, and I both feel and see Her frustration.

Their daughter is in that phase of being an older child suddenly inhabiting a woman's body in a bikini. It appears She wants to freely roam the beach.

I see each family member playing parts of an antiquated myth.

The family's collective body language is clear: Her father leans forward with chest out, domineering and overprotective. He is grabbing at Her arm, as if to hold Her down. The Mother is looking away; frustrated and obediently silent – almost as if to remove Herself from a situation She feels powerless to influence. The daughter's head hangs low in an attempt to hide Her tears – She appears defeated, dejected.

"But Daddy...?" Her voice trails off.

The situation pulls at my humanness.

As, I watch the futility of them resisting *What She Wants*, I become aware of the same resistance in me.

I know the father because he and I are the same. I too want to control and protect Her. I too want to keep things the same. I too want things to be different.

I know the Mother as well, for I recognize Her in me. I too feel unsafe, withdrawing from uncomfortable situations when I feel disempowered.

And I know the daughter perhaps best of all. I pursued Her as a younger man, and I still pursue with my eyes and imagination today.

Yes, I am that man.

I turn toward my eldest with the gold hula. She is ready to begin. She raises the hoop above Her head with great intention. Like a ballerina, She poses artistically for a few moments before Her routine.

Her stage is the beach.

The audience is all around.

They don't know they came to see Her.

But they have.

She is in the center ring, and I am sitting nearby with two obvious choices... pretending this isn't happening or trying to stop Her. But in this moment, I am recognizing a third option – to look directly into the eyes of Her creative expression – to fully be present with what is happening.

It's the same option that remains unseen to the family I just witnessed on the beach. The very door hidden by our collective fascination between right and wrong, up and down, good and bad - it exists in front of us.

It's being fully present with my daughter's emerging Goddess now that allows me to celebrate Her authentic expression.

My emotions are wild, untethered. They pull at me as though I am being quartered. I am terrified of what I am feeling and where it might lead.

Instead of reacting, I choose the *willingness* to become still with my feelings.

I make the choice to utilize Heart Vision to see Her as an Emerging Goddess – to connect to Divine Love as I am watching from my front row seat on the beach.

Looking at Her with appreciation, I gaze directly and softly at Her – while opening my heart to both the energy of the Earth and the Heavens.

Because I am this man as well.

Review
1111

Origin

See Goddess   *With Heart Vision*

Feel Her Essence

Honor Her Request

Listen from the Heart

Open to Something New

Own it Brothers & Sisters

Bring Desire to the Heart

Self Organizing Field

Radical Guide

Origin

Heart Vision:

Seeing life from innocence.

Being still with feelings while observing life unfolding.

New Language:

I AM powerfully in my feeling body knowing all is well.

Feel Her Essence

I watch Her… She is poetry in motion, graceful and elegant, and I'm not the only one noticing.

One thousand eyes it seems are suddenly watching. Young men are standing up to take a look, older men with wives and daughters are trying to appear as though they don't notice, and children are stopping what they are doing to watch the girl with the golden hula.

It becomes theatrical. There is a crowd around Her, some taking video. It is utterly beyond my control, and I am fully in it, but not a part of it. My resistance surfaces. I feel a desire to protect Her.

But from what?

Perhaps you can Appreciate Her instead.

Right… Back to my breath and my Heart.

I use the practice to go beyond my fears and judgments to connect my feelings to Her Goddess, and I am pleasantly surprised in a strange sort of way at my ability to be present with my own feelings and not react.

Somehow, by appreciating Her essence with feeling, I have entered a new normal. What I had once imagined as a terrifying situation, simply becomes what is, and I return to life on the beach. A cold beer, a sand castle, giggles with my other daughters and thoughts about lunch.

As the afternoon winds down and the sun drops into the ocean, my two younger daughters and I are packing up our beach things and getting ready to walk to our rented home in the jungle. Looking around the beach, I am curious about the whereabouts of the Hula Girl.

All the surfers hang out in a certain location, and I suspect She's there. We begin walking towards town, trusting we reconvene. We walk past the surfer's hangout. It's vacant.

We continue toward the center of town.

I must reveal to you I am feeling pretty good about myself in this moment: sun-kissed, a bit tipsy perhaps, relaxed and happy to be in Mexico and through the hula episode. For years, I had been promising my girls this experience and I was elated to be giving it to them.

In every man's life however, are the moments which suddenly emerge when his guard is down and attention elsewhere, which challenge neither his intellect nor his skill, but his ability to be present in the moment and refrain from hurtful re-action.

The implications are far reaching in these moments – and while there is no way for me to know this moment is arriving, it should have been more obvious.

I know, because I am this man. I have I used intimidating language I later regretted.

With my two younger daughters in tow, and the street full of vendors, people and maître d's trying to seat us for dinner, I am suddenly grabbed from behind.

It's the Hula Girl:

"Daddy?"

　　　"Yes?"

"I've met some new friends…"

　　　Without delay, She launches into Her evening plans.

"There is an all-night party…"

　　　I try to stay present with Her words - standing there next to my 14-year old, with one hand holding the hand of my 7-year old and the other a beach bag.

"I can stay at one of their house's."

> Whatever sense of relaxation, I had obtained by being at the beach all day has disappeared.

"They are amazing."

> I'm simply a middle-aged man with daughters and a nightmare has suddenly come true.

"They are surfers."

> I silently say, "Are you kidding me? Here in Mexico? Now?"

"Can I Daddy? – Please!"

It is clear what She wants.

What She wants is to stay out all night with a group of surfers in a foreign country.

A million judgments pass through my mind in an instant. There is a darkness pulling at me. It's angry, manipulative and feels trapped. It wants to reach out of me and put a stop to the madness.

I don't know what to do, and yet I know I must do something different. My life has brought me to this moment to make a new choice – to find the gift behind the hidden door.

I look away to survey the scene.

I need time – but there is none.

I need counsel – but there is no one.

This cannot be happening – but it is.

My younger daughters are keenly observing.

I want to say: "NO!"

But I don't.

Instead I take a deep breath into my heart and turn to face Her again.

I am becoming a new man.

○

○○○○

○○○○○○○○

Review
2222

Origin

See Goddess　　　　*With Heart Vision*

Feel Her Essence　　　***In Heart Presence***

Honor Her Request

Listen from the Heart

Open to Something New

Own it Brothers & Sisters

Bring Desire to the Heart

Self Organizing Field

Radical Guide

Origin

Heart Presence:

A relational space free of old storylines and the initiation point of manifestation using Linguistic Intelligence.

New Language:

I AM learning to allow my feelings to guide my actions.

Be completely present.

There are no other realities.

This is what is happening now.

Yes, you are the Creator of your life.

You invited this challenge to find a gift.

Now learn how to say Yes with All Your Heart.

*The Heart Presence holds no story when your energy is vertical.
What it means to have vertical energy is to connect your Heart to the
Heavens and Earth simultaneously while feeling the totality of your
feelings as completely yours.*

*It means to find 100% of your life satisfaction within.
To know Yourself as God.
IAM Divine.*

*When you learn language creates your reality, you only use words of
love.
You see potential in everything and Light in Everyone.
And therefore in You.*

Honor Her Request

3333

3+3+3+3=12

○

○○○○

○○○○○○○○

○○○○○○○○○○○○○○

Honor Her Request

Looking Her in the eyes, I ask the following:

"Is there any part of you anywhere that feels like you are in any danger?"

She pauses, closes Her eyes, and for a moment is still. I am observing Her carefully, slightly curious about Her answer and not at all surprised when it comes out.

"No Daddy, I feel good. I feel safe."

My one easy way out has just vaporized before me, and it didn't buy me much time.

"Ok then, you and your sisters go get these men and all of

you meet me in the center of the town square in 15 minutes."

"I must reveal myself to you," I say. "I am scared, I feel a lot of pressure, and your mother is not here to assist. I am going to walk around town and explore my consciousness."

"Okay Daddy," She says enthusiastically, and the three of them disappear into the afternoon dusk leaving me completely alone with my thoughts and the responsibility of making a decision with seemingly far reaching implications.

As I walk around the busy little village with people joyfully in the spirit of Christmas, I ponder the situation, and it becomes clear to me. I am expected to act on Her behalf by many people.

It's impossible to un-remember the news stories of teenage girls who disappear while on vacation, and to stop myself from entertaining the possibility of something similar happening here. I watch my mind explore multiple endings to an imaginary tragedy.

I am overwhelmed by the implications of what can possibly happen, and the scrutiny of granting permission if even the mildest of my fears manifests.

How would I explain myself to Her mother? Not to mention Her grandparents. I feel trapped and alone. Simply saying yes, doesn't feel right at all.

And what about Her sisters? It's impossible to remove them from the process of making this decision. It is literally playing out in the public square for everyone to see.

I feel the big truth too: My daughters are getting a sneak preview of their how their future romantic relationships play out with me.

I am also curious about the implications of simply saying "No," and sticking to it. There is much inside me that wants to take this route, to be protective, and to make an example for Her sisters.

Being in control is alluring to me right now, but No doesn't feel right to my Heart... so I shift my perspective by exploring the question:

How Can I Give Her What She Wants?

How Can I Say Yes?

What guides me into this new direction now is the intention my daughter and I made a few years ago about our relationship. We agreed to be transparent about our feelings and tell the truth.

For example, if She felt good about something that I didn't feel good about, She would honor my feelings, and be willing to listen. I would in turn share authentically what I was feeling.

My approach was to *never make Her wrong*.

In turn she would answer my questions transparently, while I would listen.

This allows us to explore the request a bit more, until we both arrive at the same clarity – even if it is painful.

The beauty of this agreement is that it brings us together to find the highest possibility of what is being presented in every moment. We have a track record of coming to powerful yes's and clear new directions together.

Our relationship takes powerful steps forward every time I allow myself the opportunity of finding the highest possible choice to emerge behind the hidden door.

Yes, I am this man.

Curious about all of the possibilities, I pause, look to the sky, open my arms wide and lift my face upward to connect the energy of my Heart to the Earth and the Heavens.

I make the intention to find a Choiceless Choice so everyone feels empowered regardless of the outcome.

Yes, clarity.

From this place of surrender, I ask for Divine assistance and keep my body still.

Review

3333

Origin

See Goddess   *With Heart Vision*

Feel Her Essence   *In Heart Presence*

Honor Her Request   ***Intend Choiceless Choice***

Listen from the Heart

Open to Something New

Own it Brothers & Sisters

Bring Desire to the Heart

Self Organizing Field

Radical Guide

Origin

Choiceless Choice:

When the power of love becomes greater than resistance, and empowering choices becomes clear for everyone. The Absolute YES, or a new clear direction.

New Language:

I AM saying yes to life to open the door of my Heart.

Your life experience is the sum result of your intentions.

Like arrows shot from a previous time into the Now.

Whether conscious or unconscious, these intentions fashion every aspect of life.

Yes, you are the Creator of your experience.

You are the Center of the Universe.

It all starts with you.

Always.

Now, give up control.

Allow Her to find Her discernment.

In the process, discover it more fully for you.

Let your feelings guide you through the turbulent waters into the still pond.

Hone your recognition of truth in the chaotic wild.

Find Choiceless Choice — the lion tamer of the shadow.

Listen From Heart

4444

$4+4+4+4=16$

Listen From Heart

I continue my walk around town, looking for a place that is quiet but not too far away from the square.

Fifteen minutes suddenly feels inadequate.

In this small window of time, I know I must get myself free from the rhetoric from an older paradigm to discover the truth. I know I must move beyond my fears, so that I am not reacting. I must find solace.

It is clear what She wants.

How can I, as a man, see this situation with clarity and humility so that everyone's highest best interests are served?

How can I Give Her What She Wants and keep my integrity and sense of responsibility intact?

There is a heavy-handed man in me. Ruled by fear, dogma, and conditioning, he relies on the Arrowhead Language of self-preservation as justification.

"You don't know what you are doing. Absolutely not, what would your mother think? You are unsafe. You can't take care of yourself. Bad things happen in Mexico. It's not up for discussion."

Underneath these words are unconscious thoughts. "I can't have my daughter running around in a foreign country all night long with a bunch of surfers. It's not right. What would people think?"

Yes I think these things. I am this man.

I find a bench on an out-of-the-way side street and sit down. The voices and music from the main street are less invasive here, and I close my eyes and take some deep breaths to open Heart Presence.

Searching for the eye of the hurricane spinning in my mind, I observe the thought winds circling counter clockwise.

I see how my mind is running wild with darker outcomes to create a justification for saying 'No'.

I witness my own fears about young women and sex. There is anger around being in this position in the first place. I notice my head drops, and my hands are clenched.

I am tense.

Re-posturing so my head is up and chest open, I spread my arms back, relax all my muscles, take another breath and keep going inside.

There is no model to understand, no roadmap to follow, and no solution to be found – except to follow feeling and open the Heart.

Noticing I am still thinking, I direct the concentration of my will to bring my attention to the Heart, rather than get stuck in the swirling storm of thoughts. I am breathing into my belly to feel. I dive as deep into my Heart as I can - to listen - searching for wisdom.

I recognize a familiar and oldscratchy record playing: "*I am not enough.*"

Opening the heart to the feeling holding this old story in place, I find a little crack, and go inside. Underneath the chatter of self-preservation, I feel the utter hopelessness of the situation.

As tears well up in my eyes, my chest quakes and suddenly I find myself crying. It is a time of great self-compassion, and I open my Heart to be in love with me... all of me, even the shame.

Moments later, there is nothing. No-thing is suddenly present.

The chatter of my mind becomes quiet, and I feel like I have reached the eye of the hurricane. Yes, the storm is swirling all around me, but I am the peacefulness inside. I have reached the center point of the storm. I feel I am the Center of the Universe... the initiation point of creation.

Keeping my eyes closed, I ask myself: "Where in the truth of my being do I feel She is unsafe?"

Stillness.

Relief.

Recognizing my 15 minutes is up; I stand and walk to the town square with a decision in front of me, but feeling open.

Review
4444

Origin

See Goddess   With Heart Vision

Feel Her Essence   In Heart Presence

Honor Her Request   Intend Choiceless Choice

Listen from the Heart   ***Be a Center of the Universe***

Open to Something New

Own it Brothers & Sisters

Bring Desire to the Heart

Self Organizing Field

Radical Guide

Origin

Center of the Universe:

In an infinite Universe, every person is the center point of all creation.

New Language:

I AM courageously feeling into the depths of my Heart to discover my truth.

Pause,

Listen,

Say Yes to Feeling.

What you think you want, is not desired by your Heart.

What you think She wants, is only a story.

Orient your awareness toward authentic truth.

Courageously discover what is beyond wanting.

Listen to the voice of your Heart.

Go into the vastness of uncertainty.

Yes, the spaces, of which you are most terrified, yield the greatest potentiality.

Yes, Give Her What She Wants.

Alchemy happens when you release the storyboard filters of your mind.

Let the truth emerge from a new innocence.

Listen deeply from your Heart.

This is transmutation.

This is evolution.

The vibration coming from a controlling man is rooted in shame.

Once the Heart opens, he feels the perfection of life flowing.

There is no 'Daddy' energy of having to set boundaries.

Instead, the man emerges as an Evolutionary Guide

Allowing Her to Find Her own discernment.

It is impossible to make mistakes from this place of Heart.

Radically trust She must experience what She must experience.

Can you love Her in evolutionary learning, regardless of outcome?

○
○○○○
○○○○○○○
○○○○○○○○○○○
○○○○○○○○○○○○○○○
○○○○○○○○○○○○○○○○○○

Open to Something New

5555

5+5+5+5=20

○

○○○○

○○○○○○○○

○○○○○○○○○○○○

○○○○○○○○○○○○○○○○

○○○○○○○○○○○○○○○○○○○○

Open to Something New

Walking now to the center of the town square toward the moment of truth, I spy them through the crowd before they see me.

I recognize one of the men with my daughters.

He is the top surfer on the beach: muscular, tall and handsome with an amazing smile.

This is getting more interesting by the moment.

As I get closer, I feel both the courage of my Heart, and the discomfort of the situation. I want to look away, but I cannot. My Heart is beating though my chest, and I'm doing my best to appear calm. I am aware I have lost every bit of control I thought I had. Somehow, I find comfort in this.

I notice myself in the eagerness of the surfers. Full of desire for the girl on the beach on vacation, and using charm to get what I want.

Yes, I am that man – still.

The welcoming committee: my three daughters, the surfer and his friends see me. I can feel the energy of the moment. They all know I hold the key to the remainder of their evening, and to some degree the remaining two weeks of our vacation.

Breaking from the group, the surfer steps forward and immediately shakes my hand. He looks me square in the eyes, and without hesitation or looking away says, "Thank you for meeting me. We will take wonderful care of your daughter. She is amazing, and I am blessed to have met Her."

"My parents own this business down the street and our house is one block over. Here is the address and phone number. She can stay with us for the night and have breakfast. Please feel free to come to the house anytime. Do you have any questions?"

Fascinating... He is speaking my language – and I can feel the truth in it. I happen to know his family. Not well, but well enough to know of their integrity.

An expansion of energy is happening in me, and in all of us. Everyone is smiling. Everyone's face is shiny with eyes bright.

A Christ-like energy rushes through me washing away any

lingering doubt and opening me up to a feeling of being unified with everything and everyone.

I hear myself say to them.

Go have the best time of your lives.

The Choiceless Choice had come and gone in an instant. It had presented and sucked us into the magic of the moment to all be in the **Absolute Yes**.

I watch for a moment as my Daughter skips away with Her new friends. Her ponytail bobs back and forth with the gait so familiar to me, and now so attractive to someone else.

I recognize in this moment: She is always going to be safe... She is always provided for.

She and I have been using Linguistic Intelligence for years. She has learned to trust Her Heart. She naturally connects to people who meet Her as a Goddess. There is no other way for this to turn out.

The big clue present all along was simply this: There had been no drama. She had met me in Her presence and I had met Her in mine.

Radical Trust in Heart Presence.

A new adventure has begun – for all of us. I turn, grab the hands of my other children and begin walking toward our rented home.

The decision has been Divinely made for us. It came so clear, and simple. I trust it completely.

Over two weeks, She stays out three nights and each time comes home the next morning and is present with the family. She follows through with Her agreements and ends up having incredible adventures with her new friends adding to our vacation.

For me, I witness Her power.

Seeing Her in Her power changes me... for what I see in Her, I am able to see in me. Seeing the gift of Her Divine expression, allows me to see my own.

By *Giving Her What She Wants*, I release the resistance to Her emergence, and therefore the resistance to my own emergence.

Little do I know what is set into motion. In short order, all kinds of new experiences arise requiring me to reveal myself even more completely.

Review
5555

Origin

See Goddess

Feel Her Essence

Honor Her Request

Listen from the Heart

Open to Something New

Own it Brothers & Sisters

Bring Desire to the Heart

Self Organizing Field

Radical Guide

Origin

With Heart Vision

In Heart Presence

Intend Choiceless Choice

Be a Center of the Universe

Radically Trust Life

Radical Trust:

Knowing One's Self as a Divine Creator of life experience, and honoring every One as Divine Creator of his or Her life.

New Language:

I AM the creator of the entirety of my life.

71

In this new era of WE consciousness, humans are invited to refine the way they make choices.

Act only when you feel so much harmony within your Heart that your mind is silent, and resistance obliterated.

Absolute Yes is a tremendously powerful flow of energy.

A river of light flowing in and out and through all things and people — connected to Divine Love and directed by Linguistic Intelligence.

Absolute Yes is the result of being transparent and using the Heart Language to exhibit self-compassion and authentic expression.

Only clear and empowering choices present - always providing new adventures of safety, peace, serendipity, abundance and expansive love.

Free yourself of reactive decisions and obvious choices.

There is always another option.

When you don't know which door to take.

When there is confusion in your mind.

When the options are clearly in front of you, but there is hesitation.

It is a signal to stop trying to figure out the best option and sit quietly with the energy running between the poles of choice.

Your mind doesn't need more information.

Your mind needs to get out of the way.

From a place of silence, bring a sense of neutrality to your mind by opening the heart to feeling.

Feel deeply inside everything.

It is time to listen with all your Heart.

Own it Brothers & Sisters

6666
6+6+6+6=24

○
○○○○
○○○○○○○○
○○○○○○○○○○○○
○○○○○○○○○○○○○○○○
○○○○○○○○○○○○○○○○○○○○
○○○○○○○○○○○○○○○○○○○○○○○○

Own it Brothers & Sisters

Just after the Mexico trip, the intuitive writings found in this book begin happening to me in earnest. I might be in a restaurant, having a conversation with a Goddess, or anywhere and I suddenly feel an inspiration to write. Some days, I receive four or five poems, and then other times one per week.

It is never just the words, however. The poems themselves seem to be mirroring my life experience and providing a map of sorts through my challenges. The energy flowing through me as I write these poems is powerful – and I find myself in Choiceless Choice to fully immerse myself into their wisdom.

It's a strange experience to suddenly receive poetry like these writings. It changes my relationship to everything by putting me face to face with what wants to be healed in me.

One day, having coffee with the Mother of our children, I observe myself in resistance to what She is saying. I am feeling attacked. It appears She is against me.

The backdrop of my life is unsettling.

I am living in a house in the final stages of foreclosure, my bank accounts are empty and I have very little income. Meanwhile I seductively speak about Heart Consciousness and the power to manifest anything truly desired, believing in human potential at what appears to be my own expense.

I've been caught between worlds for a few years now. Leaving behind the security our culture promises for a much different reward, I radically trust a new emergence.

The polarity present in my life is comical. On one hand I write about empowerment, and on the other I am living on the brink.

Yes, I am this man.

She relates our Hula Daughter's desire to go to college in the fall, and She wants to know about my plans for my half of the tuition.

I am feeling uncomfortable. I want to defend myself. I can feel anger rising in me.

But now, recalling my experience in Mexico, I lean back in my chair and set the intent to listen from my Heart to orient from the question of *"How Can I Give Her What She Wants"*.

Incredulously, I discover two things about myself in the next few moments. First is that I am now hearing Her words as requests rather than attacks. Secondly, I become present in a way I've never been before that my stories are only as true as I believe them to be.

What a humbling experience to recognize in a flash the woman before me is communicating in ways I have been inept to follow. Now, simply owning my life instead of defending myself shifts everything.

In this moment, I choose to take Her medicine. A new truth emerges. I can hear She wants the best for me. She believes in me. I see the Goddess in Her. I feel new possibilities. By taking Her medicine, I am ready to take my own.

A week later with our Hula Girl, the three of us sit at a small table in the same coffee shop.

"Mom & Dad?"

    "Yes?"

"I've decided on college…"

    Without delay, She launches into Her college plans.

"I'm only applying to one school – if I don't get in, so be it."

    I try to stay present with Her words, sitting there across from Her Mother aware this isn't going quite like we'd imagined.

"There is this amazing school in Florida."

> It feels to me time has suddenly compressed and we are all sitting under a microscope.

"It's a private school."

> I'm simply a middle-aged divorced man living on the brink and a great gift has suddenly emerged.

It is clear what She wants.

What She wants is to go to high-end private college 2,000 miles away.

As Her Mother and I digest this new information, our Hula Girl sits in Her chair patiently awaiting Her parents to own the magic She has always known, "I create what my Heart desires."

In the uncomfortable silence that ensues, old dynamics of our marital relationship beckon, but not like they used to. Some vulnerability surfaces and is expressed. However, it soon becomes clear we have an opportunity to demonstrate our power by living a new story through our collective Heart Presence.

Suddenly, there is no opposition to Her request, and the three of us orient from the power of our intent rather than the present state of affairs. We choose to radically trust all is being provided for Her. It feels like a vacuum sucks the remaining tension from the room. Suddenly we are in love, again.

We stand and face one another and set the intention from this place of excitement – we don't know how it's all happening, we simply agree it is happening: She is getting in and all the required resources become available.

It's an Absolute Yes.

Some months later, we are all enjoying the Hula Girl's high school graduation celebration and her upcoming fall semester at her school of choice at my new home by the river. Not only has She gotten what She wants, it seems like we all have.

I have arrived back at a home I once lived. It's an extraordinary parcel of land with a beautiful winding waterway. Large Cottonwood trees frame an unobstructed view of the mountains to the west. There is abundant land for gardens on the other side of river. From the pedestrian bridge, I often stand above the flow looking upriver to reflect on how life continues to create itself around my intent, from the Center of my Universe.

Four years before, I left my marriage to move into this house with another woman after receiving a vision for starting a community. I built a labyrinth and wrote The Evolutionary Guidebook here.

Now the extended family has gathered here to celebrate in love. It is our home.

Yes, I am that man. I did that. All of it.

Standing on the bridge, I gaze into the mountains beyond the bend of the river. None of this makes any rational sense at all, and yet it feels right to my Heart. I am inspired to keep saying yes, despite how uncomfortable I often feel.

My intuition is strong in this moment, and unsettling to me. I feel is time to start a MysterE School by inviting two women to join me in establishing a community dedicated to exploring human potentiality. They are half my age.

When I met them, there is an instant connection with both. In their eyes, Light is dancing. In their Hearts, love is present. In their language, a curiosity to explore life. They are enthusiastically pursuing a greater truth.

One woman desires to open to Her gift of music, and find Her voice on stage. The other desires to share Her gift for permaculture and education by starting a children's nature school. They are both interested in living in and co-creating a new paradigm.

It's an Absolute Yes, and a community is born.

Concurrently contrast emerges in my life. Following through with this means I have to fully own at the age of 47, I have housemates close to my Hula Daughter's age. Life is different, suddenly. This truth I recognize is terrifying to me in terms of public perception, and I see it strokes my ego as well.

My lifestyle creates reactions. One afternoon over coffee, a woman close to me says: "Maybe you ought to keep your pants on for a while."

I hear what She is saying to me, and I feel She is sharing far more than Her perspective – She is sharing Divine Truth to support my intent of being in right relationship so these women feel safe enough to emerge into their gifts.

I catch myself in the awareness of being a man I once chastised. Seeing my raw humanness in the face of it, I vow to take my physical needs out of the equation of all relationships until there is an Absolute Yes for the next intimate partner.

I am this man.

The months roll by quickly. The community develops a cohesive and empowered relational field by practicing *Give Her What She Wants*.

Many new Centers of the Universe are showing up attracted to the vibrant energy of the River House MysterE School. Something is happening here people can tangibly feel. The more we collectively say Yes, the easier it is to trust our magic.

When these new people arrive, there is an instant connection. In their eyes, light is dancing. In their Hearts, love is present. In their language, a curiosity to explore life. They are enthusiastically pursuing a greater truth.

They are inspired by the music and the prospect of a new school for children. They come and sit in Heart Presence on the bank of the river to share their dreams and speak the

Heart Language. They have been looking for a place to call home and open to the magic inherent to their Hearts.

We are learning to say Yes to the gift of life in all Her many forms, especially in terms of relating to one another.

We are noticing, when we say Yes, the people to whom we are relating either step more fully into an empowered relationship with us, or naturally take themselves elsewhere.

We also notice how the absence of competitiveness and division allows us to be in a powerful manifesting vortex, enabling us all to get what we all want.

A collective vision emerges and everyone sees how each individual gift plays a vital role.

More people say Yes.

Inspiration guides action.

Beautiful healthy meals are prepared.

Community projects are born and advance quickly.

Gardens are created, classes are taught, books are written.

Children are at school in the day and the band plays at night.

Anything has become possible.

Review

6666

Origin

See Goddess

With Heart Vision

Feel Her Essence

In Heart Presence

Honor Her Request

Intend Choiceless Choice

Listen from the Heart

Be a Center of the Universe

Open to Something New

Radically Trust Life

Own it Brothers & Sisters

We are Alchemists

Bring Desire to the Heart

Self Organizing Field

Radical Guide

Origin

Alchemy:

When two or more Centers of the Universe align with shared intent in Heart Presence, they open higher dimensions of consciousness for transformation and manifestation.

New Language:

I AM sharing my magic with others in Heart Presence.

Speak your truth.

Own your darker side.

Come clean on your secrets.

Communicate your needs to others.

Create negative space inside with forgiveness.

All you have to do is reveal yourself in Radical Trust.

Increase your manifesting power by using the Heart Language.

The human constellation cares for everything when you are transparent.

A most compassionate action is allow dramatic relationships to naturally fade away.

You are meeting new brothers and sisters for a reason.

These relationships are far more potent in Heart Presence.

Clean it up with your ex-lovers so a harmonic field exists for All.

It is Happening. *Heart Language*
based relationships are so *magically and amazingly*
transformative, people naturally *are inspired to live harmoniously*
in proximity, causing compassionate *fun communities to naturally form.*
Yes, these communities are so attractive, that more and more people join
and extend outward to start new like-Hearted communities. These
"Yes Communities" create enlightened pockets of reality in
societies that quickly grow, invisibly shifting
human consciousness from within,
like transformation of
caterpillars into
butterflies.
Yes.

And   then,

When the   influence

of your outdated   language fades,

And the Heart communities connect and merge as One,

Everyone will know what the Goddess already knows,

All is Provided For Now.

We Can All Get What We All Want.

○

○○○○

○○○○○○○○

○○○○○○○○○○○○

○○○○○○○○○○○○○○○○

○○○○○○○○○○○○○○○○○○○○

○○○○○○○○○○○○○○○○○○○○○○○○

○
○○○○
○○○○○○○
○○○○○○○○○○○
○○○○○○○○○○○○○○○
○○○○○○○○○○○○○○○○○○○
○○○○○○○○○○○○○○○○○○○○○○○
○○○○○○○○○○○○○○○○○○○○○○○○○○○

Bring Desire to the Heart

7777
$7+7+7+7 = 28$

○

○○○○

○○○○○○○

○○○○○○○○○○

○○○○○○○○○○○○○

○○○○○○○○○○○○○○○○

○○○○○○○○○○○○○○○○○○○

○○○○○○○○○○○○○○○○○○○○○○

○○○○○○○○○○○○○○○○○○○○○○○○○

Bring Desire to Heart

A beautiful community friend and Goddess asks me to go to a party in an unfamiliar place, in another town. Despite being out of my comfort zone, the opportunity feels right and I notice how my schedule suddenly frees up the necessary time and arrangements.

She is clear with me on Her intent. We are going together, but separately. She desires to meet someone. When that happens, I am on my own. Furthermore, She wants to stay out all night and requests me to be available to drive Her back in the morning.

Feeling into whether or not this is an Absolute Yes, I sit in the mystery of my Heart and listen to the feelings.

Is this where I am being asked to go?

Discover freedom in Love.

Become free in what you dream for.

And become free with what shows up in your dream.

Have Radical Trust in the Mystery.

She and I go on incredible adventures together. But, when She arrives to pick me up there isn't enough clarity for an Absolute Yes, and I have yet to get ready for the event.

I say to Her: "I still don't have an Absolute Yes on this one, can you help me get there?"

Taking my hands in Hers, She meets my gaze. She asks, "Sure Babe, what are you feeling?"

I express my vulnerability about being unsure of going to a place of not knowing anyone and potentially staying out all night depending on Her whims.

I can feel Her listening with me. Her eyes comfort me with a soft willingness to be open to what is transpiring. She is a sovereign woman, and flows with the moment beautifully.

After a pause, she states:

"I have a feeling it is important for you to come with me, and I want that," she says. "But more than that, I am here to support whatever choice you need to make in this moment. I am having an amazing time whether you come or not!"

"I am not sure I want to end up alone at 3:00 am away from home," I say.

"Then don't!" She says.

A perfect reflection of Self-realization from the Goddess. My experience is completely up to me.

Align your language carefully with the Heart,
And BE careful what you wish for.

A Goddess is not looking for a life partner.
She is looking for partners in life.

Giving voice to my fears, I am suddenly relieved of them – and I notice how I share Her intent. Standing with Her, I open to the feeling of a Heart connection, tonight.

It's an uncomfortable rush of energy rushing through me for a moment as it washes the fears away. "I am ready to meet someone too," I say. "It's feels like it is time."

We smile together, and it becomes clear.

"Help me pick out something to wear," I say laughing. "Seems like a good opportunity to let a Goddess dress me."

It's an Absolute Yes.

Master the art of creating from nothing,

Trust the oldest spiritual law:

Everything comes from the space of nothingness.

Yes, no-thing is inside of you.

Open the door of the Heart into the emptiness of nothing.

Open to the Absolute Yes. It's a Big Bang.

Arriving and moving from room to room, I notice this party has attracted many people like me. I feel comfortable here and I open to the music and gaiety of the gathering. The conversation is beautiful and empowering with everyone. In their eyes, light is dancing. In their Hearts, love is present. In their language, a curiosity to explore life.

When the Goddess shows up is completely up to you.

Who, what, where & how She does, is not.

Take your loneliness and your human desires to the fire and incinerate them.

The moment you release your needs on the horizontal or conditional level, the Goddess appears next to you fireside as if by magic.

Although She offers no potions, be sure She carries the exact medicine your awakening requires.

Open your Heart to Her Essence.

There is a crowd of people outside by the fire. The house is thumping with music and dancing. It's a seamless chemistry experiment of Heart, and I am enjoying the ride. Suddenly, everyone goes inside to dance, and I am inspired to stay by the fire – alone.

It's 3:00am, and I notice I am exactly where I imagined myself to be earlier.

Acknowledging an old story of 'being alone' that wants my attention, I open my Heart up to 'being all-one" instead. I begin rolling some tobacco.

Moments later, while reaching into my jeans pocket for the lighter, I angle my chin to put the cigarette to my mouth and my gaze shifts upward.

I notice Her first, waltzing across the lawn. Her feet seem to be barely touching the ground.

I feel Divine Orchestration at play.

I strike the lighter and take a deep drag.

We are now noticing each other in the shortening space between us. She is waltzing. I am still, watching. We are smiling. She stands beside me for a long moment.

I bid a chair.

She sits instead on the bench next to me surrounded by many empty seats.

In Her eyes, light is dancing. In Her Heart, love is present. She is enthusiastically sharing Her truth.

We are speaking the same language.

Your receptivity has invited Her into your Heart, igniting the sacred twin fires.

You have begun a journey into potentiality previously unknown.

Dive deeper into the fire, and keep saying Yes.

There is ease in the way we have found one another. Like a beautiful flowing river, the conversation flows gracefully, enveloping us in a point of richness beneath the cascading love. She is singing Her Heart Song, and I am listening deeply, inebriated in love.

Hours pass instantly, and as the sun is rising, my friend who invited me on this journey arrives to the fire. It is time to go.

We stand. In our embrace we begin to have a shared experience of sensuality moving through us beckoning more connection.

"Do you feel that?" She asks, looking intently in my eyes.

"Yes," I respond. "Can you bring it to your Heart?"

I sense Her soften a little and the space between our eyes becomes fuzzy. What once was a distinct sexual desire becomes an expansive feeling of connectivity which envelopes us both.

She became in that moment, everything my Heart desired.

It's an Absolute Yes. Alchemy.

Pulling back from a long embrace, I gaze into Her eyes for a moment and smiling I say, "Goodnight, what a pleasure."

Then, She went back to Her life, and I went back to mine.

Divine Orchestration indeed.

○

○○○○

○○○○○○○

○○○○○○○○○○

○○○○○○○○○○○○○

○○○○○○○○○○○○○○○○

○○○○○○○○○○○○○○○○○○○

○○○○○○○○○○○○○○○○○○○○○○

Review
7777

Origin

See Goddess | With Heart Vision

Feel Her Essence | In Heart Presence

Honor Her Request | Intend Choiceless Choice

Listen from the Heart | Be a Center of the Universe

Open to Something New | Radically Trust Life

Own it Brothers & Sisters | We are Alchemists

Bring Desire to the Heart | **For Divine Orchestration**

Self Organizing Field

Radical Guide

Origin

Divine Orchestration:

The path of serendipity flowing to Absolute Yes. Everything working out better than anyone could have planned.

New Language:

I AM fully in my Heart with all of my desire.

Know Your

Truth

The highest integrity of relationship is created from Absolute Twin Yes.

She becomes One you love, until the mission with Her is over.

It may be 7 minutes, 7 months, 7 years or 7 decades.

Now, stop projecting She is the One.

And become the One for Her.

Yes, You are the One.

It is up to you.

Life is a gift.

Keep on gifting.

Express appreciation.

And then give some more.

Open the back of your Heart.

And receive the Divine Goddess.

Everything you desire is already here.

Don't go looking for it.

Give It a Way.

Now.

Give it away from within and open to receive.

Your life is all about healing.

Which is to say the dissolution of all things but the Divine God in you.

Give Her What She wants until there is nothing left but this truth.

Give Her What She Wants Until You are completely empty.

*And then give Her more, until the Back of Your
Heart is wide open and there is nothing but
negative space.*

Become nothing to obtain everything.

Eradicate the desire to succeed.

There is nothing there.

It is the thrusting that must be softened now.

Become receptive.

It is already here, now.

Align language with the Heart,

And BE very careful what you wish for.

All is Provided For Now.

○
○○○○
○○○○○○○
○○○○○○○○○○
○○○○○○○○○○○○○
○○○○○○○○○○○○○○○○
○○○○○○○○○○○○○○○○○○○
○○○○○○○○○○○○○○○○○○○○○○
○○○○○○○○○○○○○○○○○○○○○○○○○

Self-Organizing

8888

$8+8+8+8 = 32$

○

○○○○

○○○○○○○

○○○○○○○○○○○

○○○○○○○○○○○○○○○

○○○○○○○○○○○○○○○○○○○

○○○○○○○○○○○○○○○○○○○○○○○

○○○○○○○○○○○○○○○○○○○○○○○○○○○

○○○○○○○○○○○○○○○○○○○○○○○○○○○○○○○

Self-Organizing

At the end of writing *Give Her What She Wants*, I call the Hula Girl on the phone.

"People want to know what happens in your life, what would you like to tell them?" I inquire. "I'm not clear yet on how this book comes to a close. How do I end a story which is just beginning?"

For nearly a year, this book has been coming into focus.

In the meantime, our community has grown substantially. We are inspired. Hope and optimism are building. We are connecting to other similar communities. Our collective way of life is inspiring others.

107

Also in this moment, I feel pressed to the very edge of my existence, feeling somehow responsible for what is happening, and not in control at all. I feel as though I am teetering on the brink and nothing is guaranteed.

My greatest fear as an author is I am making everything up, and I'll turn out the fool because it didn't really work out the way I planned – therefore disappointing others and validating my human story – of not being enough.

But that's not the Hula Girl's experience.

She says to me: "What I have noticed Dad, is that many of the friends I am making in college are stuck in power dynamics with their fathers. They are either rebelling against them and/or trying to please them, which colors the way they see life with story."

"But in our relationship, I know I am always free to make my own choices and you trust I am creating my life in the way I am inspired. That changes everything. My life is amazing, everything is getting better and better. It's really wild, everything I require to thrive keeps showing up."

"You've always been a great teacher for me," I reply. "I remember years ago when I became aware of your magic. Thank you for being so patient with me."

'No problem Dad," She says laughing.

"By the way, the band is playing on the night of the book release. How would you like to hula on stage in a red dress? I can fly you in for the weekend."

Without delay, She launches into Her plans for the trip.

"Really Daddy!? Can I bring a friend?"

It's an Absolute Yes.

My willingness to listen to Her re-orients me back to my Heart.

I am inspired to speak to myself compassionately, and I share my vulnerability of releasing this book with my community to dispel my old storylines. With compassion for Me, I open to new perspectives with curiosity:

Perhaps, I am emerging into something beyond what I can imagine and the fear is not fear at all. Perhaps the fear is simply the energy required to make a shift in my evolution bumping up against my old stories. Perhaps everything is perfectly perfect just the way it is.

When The Evolutionary Guidebook: Follow Your Heart and BE Your Power emerged from my Heart in 2009, I had no idea how impactful a change in consciousness could be.

That book too, took me right to the edge. All I could do was to invite people to explore their Heart while I did the same.

And now five years later, I am a Center of the Universe in the middle of something extraordinary. Its potency I feel, we are just beginning to appreciate. I couldn't have planned any of this and yet, I am amongst a growing group of people answering the call of their Hearts.

It's a compassionate movement. We are answering the collective emergence of the One Heart - the Earth's call for Feminine Leadership.

Feminine Leadership:

The Allowance of Emergence, or Alchemy.

Feminine Leadership's essence is this question:

> *Does everyone feel safe enough to authentically express themselves in their gift, and is the relational field harmonious enough to allow for the natural order of life to reveal itself perfectly in every moment to support the sovereignty of the individuals and the collective empowerment of the community and beyond?*

In Feminine Leadership, everyone is in agreement to be in service of His or Her gift and to allow the Feminine element of compassion to guide from this truth:

> *When people are aligned in the Heart.*
>
> *All is Provided for Now*

And yet, we are living in a world of absolute paradox. Humanity is in extreme polarity. It's good against evil, right

110

against wrong, red against blue, rich against poor.

People are feeling pressed to the very edge of human existence, feeling somehow responsible for what is happening, and not in control at all. We feel as though we are teetering on the brink and nothing is guaranteed.

Is it possible, we have been led to the edge of existence to emerge into something beyond what we can imagine?

The signs are all around us. Can you recognize them?

There is fear and chaos in our minds as the old stories get loud. Relationships are shifting with accompanying drama. We feel pressure, the backs of our Hearts are aching and there is a presence of strong energy. Our addictions pull at us. We see choice in terms of polarity – a right and a wrong. We are trying to fix problems.

Honor Human Intimacy.

Free yourself from shame.

Reveal yourself and stand in Your Truth.

Emerge into Your God Self.

You are Divine.

The Hula Girl is revealing to me that Freedom of Expression is the hidden doorway.

Her freedom of expressing what She is feeling allows Her to

live in the moment. She becomes the Center of the Universe when She is fully alive in Her Self. Everything gets better and better for Her because She is allowing Her Heart to write the story of Her life. She knows Herself as a Goddess. She recognizes Her own Divinity.

Now, here on the phone, I am seeing the reflection of Me in Her, again.

I am now in the knowingness, as I allow my Self to freely express, the book finishes itself easefully. The story becomes what is happening, rather what I want to happen, or fear might happen. I am simply one human expression, and yet I am experiencing my Self as a God. I am recognizing my own Divinity.

My pathway becomes illuminated as I express what my Heart desires, and everything gets better and better. I am allowing My Heart to write the story of my life.

I am responsible to My Heart's desire.

I choose to Radically Trust.

I am that Man.

Are You?

I invite you to observe the language you are speaking, and hearing in your life. Seemingly, humanity is against one another right now, frantically looking for the safer side to join. No one wants to be without a chair when the music stops.

What is the <u>O</u>rigin of this language - compassion or something else?

Experience tells me the Goddess emerges when She feels safe enough in Her expression.

She is no longer interested in being the object of lust. She is no longer interested in playing in a conditional reality game of love and affection. She is no longer interested in living within the boundaries we men have created. She is no longer interested in men who keep secrets.

It is our responsibility therefore, as men to create a safe space for the Goddess to emerge in all of us.

To become a man of Feminine Leadership, I invite you to play a new game. A game where the music never stops and there is always a chair for everyone. A game where the answer is always "Yes." A game where relationships live in the moment rather than by expectation, definition and old storylines. A game where every person is honored as Divine, even You.

Yes, that's the big truth we men have been too afraid to see. Each of us is Divine. We are Gods. And, we each have a map showing us how to stand in our power to serve the Feminine in the ways of nurture, nature and creativity.

In the freedom of Self-expression, the Heart becomes our teacher, and the Heart becomes our guide, and we are individually and collectively empowered in this choice.

In doing so, we ALL thrive.

It's right in front of us... and always has been. We have neither failed nor succeeded as men. We are simply evolving, as we have always done.

We are these men.

We are emerging in our new truth:

We are Radical Guides for Human Evolution.

YES

Say YES to life.

Say YES to Heart's Desire.

We Can ALL Get What We ALL Want

Say YES to Heart's Desire.

Say YES to life.

YES

○

○○○○

○○○○○○○

○○○○○○○○○○

○○○○○○○○○○○○○

○○○○○○○○○○○○○○○○

○○○○○○○○○○○○○○○○○○○

○○○○○○○○○○○○○○○○○○○○○○

○○○○○○○○○○○○○○○○○○○○○○○○○

○○○○○○○○○○○○○○○○○○○○○○○○○○○○

Review

8888

Origin

See Goddess

With Heart Vision

Feel Her Essence

In Heart Presence

Honor Her Request

Intend Choiceless Choice

Listen from the Heart

Be a Center of the Universe

Open to Something New

Radically Trust Life

Own it Brothers & Sisters

We are Alchemists

Bring Desire to the Heart

For Divine Orchestration

Self Organizing Field

With Intent to Heal

Radical Guide

Origin

<u>The Intent for Healing</u>:

Seeing life as presenting reflections in every moment for healing, so the Universe can give what is required for life.

<u>New Language</u>:

I AM in the appreciation of my life Self-organizing around the quality of my intent bringing me what I require to thrive.

117

Appreciation,

is the mechanism that allows Humanity to balance immediately.

There is no reason to be in judgment of anyone.

There is no reason to exercise any agenda or control.

Being against anything at any level only reinforces that condition.

At this moment in human history, it is a time to let go completely of all ideas, plans, and constructs about fixing or solving any problems.

Trusting in Divine perfection rather than perspective is the mechanism.

Feeling self-compassion in every moment activates the mechanism.

The world isn't what it appears to be from a conditional perspective.

When you are in the Heart, you are aware that everything is connected.

Divine Love allows everything to exist in the form it currently exists.

Politics, religion, environment, technology, warlords, priests, Her & You

To bring anything into harmony with its potential, you simply love it.

Simply BE in Heart Presence with everything.

Turn your attention to the Heart.

Especially Her's.

When you love what is, regardless of perspective, you alchemize potential.

Potential is everything's most Divine expression.

Use the mirror, and love what bothers you the most.

Appreciation,

is the mechanism that allows Humanity to balance immediately.

Leaders in

every level of consciousness

are helping to hold each level together in

government, religion, commerce, education, transportation,

security, medical, monetary and communication institutions.

It's important to have leadership in those levels.

Judging them heats up the pot, adding pressure.

Change under pressure becomes destructive.

Things allowed to evolve; shift gracefully.

All levels are reflections of your human consciousness.

7 billion centers of the Universe reflecting in the mirror.

Everyone is exactly where they are supposed to be.

Everything is Divinely placed.

It's already all perfect.

So love what is.

Discard your stories.

Use the mirror to see what to love.

Keep loving until it is All Love.

Be Your Radical Guide

9999
$9+9+9+9 = 36$

MASCULINE

9

9 9 9

Be Your

$9+9+9+9= 36$

Radical Guide

LIFE IS A PERFECT MIRROR

Everything you think is only 180 degrees of it

Embody your feminine perspective of self-compassion

The heart offers experience of complimentary perspective

Complete the sphere. Become THE Center of Your Universe

$$0+0+0+0=O$$
$$1+1+1+1=4$$
$$2+2+2+2=8$$
$$3+3+3+3=12$$
$$4+4+4+4=16$$
$$5+5+5+5=20$$
$$6+6+6+6=24$$
$$7+7+7+7=28$$
$$8+8+8+8=32$$
$$\underline{9+9+9+9= 36}$$
$$= 180$$

= 180 Degrees or ½ of Perspective

9

9 9 9

Be Your

9+9+9+9= 36

Radical Guide

LIFE IS A PERFECT MIRROR

Everything you think is only 180 degrees of it
Embody your feminine perspective of self-compassion
The heart offers experience of complimentary perspective
Complete the sphere. Become THE Center of Your Universe

$$0+0+0+0=O$$
$$1+1+1+1=4$$
$$2+2+2+2=8$$
$$3+3+3+3=12$$
$$4+4+4+4=16$$
$$5+5+5+5=20$$
$$6+6+6+6=24$$
$$7+7+7+7=28$$
$$8+8+8+8=32$$
$$\underline{9+9+9+9= 36}$$
$$= 180$$

(compassion)

ADD FEMININE

EQUALS THE MIRROR

○
○○○○
○○○○○○○
○○○○○○○○○○
○○○○○○○○○○○○○
○○○○○○○○○○○○○○○○
○○○○○○○○○○○○○○○○○○○
○○○○○○○○○○○○○○○○○○○○○○
○○○○○○○○○○○○○○○○○○○○○○○○○
○○○○○○○○○○○○○○○○○○○○○○○○○○○○
○○○○○○○○○○○○○○○○○○○○○○○○○○○○○○
○○○○○○○○○○○○○○○○○○○○○○○○○○○○○○
○○○○○○○○○○○○○○○○○○○○○○○○○○○
○○○○○○○○○○○○○○○○○○○○○○○○
○○○○○○○○○○○○○○○○○○○○○
○○○○○○○○○○○○○○○○○○
○○○○○○○○○○○○○○○
○○○○○○○○○○○○
○○○○○○○
○○○○
○

Yes.

Looking

at life without

compassion reveals ½

of the map. Add compassion

to reveal the total map.

The map is the

Mirror.

Yes.

Be Your Radical Guide.

Be Your Radical Guide

I spent seven years with a spiritual teacher. It was in His Heart Presence that I discovered a spiritual desire to open my Heart.

I prayed, commanded, begged and pleaded with God for the gift of an open Heart. I practiced with incredible desire.

Then one night in a dream, a Swami kidnapped me in a 1960's era VW hippy bus, and driving like a complete lunatic took me to a vacant stretch of highway.

Screeching to a halt, I was thrown into the summer grass on my back on the shoulder of the road. Then straddling me, he cut open my chest and took out my Heart in his bare hand. Reaching above me he handed my old Heart to my dead mother, who then gave the Swami a new Heart for me. He then placed the new Heart in my chest and sewed me up with Light.

Does it get any more radical than that?

Things in my reality began shifting rather quickly, including leaving my teacher. Now, I find myself in a vastly different reality. I now recognize all of life as the spiritual teacher, including every person with whom I interact. It's quite magical.

All of life is the mirror of Me.

I experience my Heart as always directing extraordinary theater, and I recognize the freewill to step into an ever-present slipstream of energy guiding me into potential, or not.

However, to evolve into potential with this energy is to be in the deep willingness to go beyond suffering.

I don't say these words lightly.

Many brothers and sisters on this planet are in pain. Prayers for everyone in pain - always. Pain is an incredible teacher.

The point of the story is this:

When you want your truth, You desire it with all your Heart. You are completely dedicated to opening your Heart, and going beyond suffering into awakening by dedicating your life to finding the Absolute Yes for you.

First, open the Heart by learning to say yes to everything, including your fears, pain and shame – your suffering.

Yes, there is an unseen door. There is a way through the pain that is evolutionary efficient and available to anyone feeling the call to awaken.

No one is opening this door for you.

It is You who rises into empowerment by having the courage to open the door by looking into the Mirror of your Heart.

Saying yes to life draws you in like water funneling into a drain. It is your appreciation of everything being presented to you that quickens the spiraling. It is your Heart Presence that allows an accelerated transformation to occur as you are swept into the vortex by engaging with the Absolute Yes.

Spiritual awareness which used to take many years, even decades, of dedicated practices to cultivate, is now happening in much smaller time increments, especially in communities of people communicating with the Heart Language.

Anything is possible now.

As you are reading these words, perhaps something inside you has become curious. Maybe you suspect our reality is far more expansive than what your five senses report, your worldview has become slightly altered and you are feeling inspired to go on a journey, into the Heart.

But perhaps you also feel scared and unsure.

I appreciate that.

Your

Fears are:

Will I lose Her?

How can I trust Her?

Is She more than I can handle?

What if She gets an addiction or more?

But this is only half the mirror. Being

Your Radical Guide is having the

guts to see your Self in

the reflection

of Her.

Own

What You See

In the Mirror of Life

to allow healing to happen.

My

Fears are.

Will I lose Me?

How can I trust Me?

Am I more than I can handle?

What if I develop addiction or more?

Saying yes to Her releases resistance in you.

The resistance of feeling your shame,

Masculine sexual shame.

Your Shadow &

Pain.

It

Is Loving

Your Shame Basket

Which Opens The Unseen Door

Allowing Everyone to Get What They Want.

Yes, life is perfect mirror. We see an exact reflection of us.

When I orient from this perfection, it's easier to see the flaws. I have learned to see these contrasts as beautiful gifts, reflecting back to me opportunities for healing. Appreciating everything I see in the mirror of life allows me to become the Center of My Universe and use the levers of my Heart to shift my experience to move into my truth:

Take a moment to sit with your Self and listen. What is your life saying to you? What words are coming out of the mouths of the women in your life? What is bothersome and painful?

Record your observations on the blank mirror, and then read the poems on the following pages, adding reflections to your mirror as inspired.

At the end of the Radical Guide, look into the mirror. Open your Heart with compassion to the Divine Reflection of You. Love what you find.

And then, one night in a dream, or under the stars, or by the fire, or standing in line for coffee, everything shifts and you awaken to a new Heart. Suddenly you notice everything you have ever wanted is magically manifesting in front of your eyes... and furthermore, you step in the recognition it was always happening that way.

Thank you for reading *Give Her What She Wants*. For a more complete version of the Radical Guide visit our online MysterE School, and accept our invitation to take a complimentary course on Heart Language / Heart Presence.

www.giveherwhatshewants.com/radical

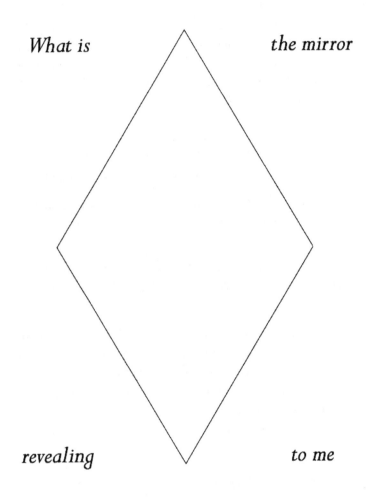

What is   *the mirror*

revealing   *to me*

○

○○○○

○○○○○○○

○○○○○○○○○○

○○○○○○○○○○○○○

○○○○○○○○○○○○○○○○

○○○○○○○○○○○○○○○○○○○

○○○○○○○○○○○○○○○○○○○○○○

○○○○○○○○○○○○○○○○○○○○○○○○○

○○○○○○○○○○○○○○○○○○○○○○○○○○○○

○○○○○○○○○○○○○○○○○○○○○○○○○○○○○○○

○○○○○○○○○○○○○○○○○○○○○○○○○○○○○○○

○○○○○○○○○○○○○○○○○○○○○○○○○○○○

○○○○○○○○○○○○○○○○○○○○○○○○○

○○○○○○○○○○○○○○○○○○○○○○

○○○○○○○○○○○○○○○○○○○

○○○○○○○○○○○○○○○○

○○○○○○○○○○○○○

○○○○○○○○○○

○○○○○○○

○○○○

○

Radical Guide

Seeds

Impregnate

the Earth's desire

to sustain life.

Earth

is nurture and nature for growth and abundance, naturally.

A man's seed impregnates the feminine desire to give and sustain life.

Woman is nurture and nature for the child, naturally.

When a woman feels something inside Her Heart,

a process of self-expression has been initiated.

She is pregnant with desire, naturally.

There is nothing you can do to stop this.

This is the most powerful source of energy known.

A woman may ignore or hide this feeling for some time.

However, Her Heart's desire is ultimately stronger than human will.

Unmet, Her desire is a disturbing force for shattering agreements.

So you might as well Give Her What She Wants right now.

You might as well align yourself with Her emergence.

Or She will quickly find a more willing partner.

THE MIRROR:

Yes,

I Give to Me,

When I Give to Her.

What I see in Her, I see in me.

She is the perfect mirror of Divine Love.

When my presence produces harmony, I AM aligned.

When my presence reveals static, it's time to look within to heal.

When my presence reveals static, it's time to look within to heal.

When my presence produces harmony, I AM in aligned.

Likewise, all of life is a mirror of Divine Love.

What I see in Life, I see in me.

When I Give to Life,

I Give to Me,

Yes.

100%
RESPONSIBILITY:

A man responsible for his life and healing, lives a Paradox:
He is powerfully in charge of his intent and energy owning 100%
responsibility for his life experiences, yet he exercises 0% control.

She cannot sing from Her Heart until She feels safe enough.
You have the capacity to open to that place for another.

First, master the Heart Presence in Your Self.
Open beyond limits of perspective.

An instant feel and it's gone.
A healing happens.

Absolute

Yes

GIVING IT TO HER

Neither wanting nor needing anything in return, Say to your beloved

"If it is in my power to give it to you, I gift through Divine Love.

I give it to you now with pure blessings of empowerment.

I am investing in your joy, Light and well-being."

All human beings desire to be met in Love.

Now, Give Her What She Wants,

Do it completely with Love.

In the Absolute Yes.

You gift Her.

Always.

Yes

Yes

Yes

Yes

Yes

Thank you. Thank you. Thank you.

HEART PRESENCE:

Healing happens purely by Heart Presence.

When two hearts come together in Absolute Yes,

Trust becomes the looking glass into new human reality.

Love is the merging of the new consciousness with the old.

The   Holy   Grail.

You have offered the gift of the element of compassion to Her.

If She remains joyful now, Give Her more of What She Wants.

If drama enters the field, step back and create some space.

Investigate with your feelings as to what is happening.

"IAM not in control of what is happening,

but I am responsible.

What is my

relationship

to the drama?"

Stay in Heart Presence.

Stay above the drama unfolding.

Let Her fall into the empty space of Her tears.

Manifest truth through the exploration of emptiness.

The man holding the mirror allowing Her to purify is purified.

NOT GIVING TO HER

When you give Her what She wants and it doesn't feel right.
What in the next step?

Ask your heart for a clear sign to know the truth.
Then follow intuitive Heart guidance.
The Universe is transparent.
She answers directly
to Heart's
inquiry.

This request is always answered.
If you cannot give Her with Love, You cannot give it to Her freely.
You are in judgment and fear, or you have been enlightened
that what She wants is poisonous.

Either way it is no longer an Absolute Yes.
Now become devoted to Give Her What She Really Wants.
From here invite Her into your Heart Presence.
Meet Her there and See Her Goddess.

MIRROR ADDICTION

The

key to breaking

addiction is to find the mirror

image of the addiction itself in one primary

relationship in your life. There is one relationship in every

awakening person that mirrors the energetic pattern of the addiction

cycle they wish to transform.

When you try to change a

relationship dynamic or heal an addiction by itself, there is actually

a huge opportunity to heal both at the same time. Although

it appears that meeting two challenges at

once would be harder, it works

exactly in the opposite

way.

ADDICTION MIRROR

By being willing to face the addiction cycle and the disempowering relationship together, you go more quickly and with greater power to the source of both (which is the same.) By appreciating the denser energies of both situations, you create an amplification of potential by allowing polarity to create a form of evolutionary fusion. This radical allowance brings in white light & energy for transformation.

From this point, you are able to practice deeper levels of forgiveness and see how you created both situations as a perfect challenge to help you awaken. You can see how it's perfectly perfect and a gift of Divine Love.

Look at the entire mosaic. Feel deeply everything. Be clear and precise with your action as guided by the heart to relieve yourself of self-sabotage. Use your community and be in love with your life to get the perspective and courage you need to take on what appears to be a great challenge, but is in truth an extraordinary gift. Finding the gift is simply a slight shift of the dial. Use the levers in your Heart.

Heart Language is about creating sovereignty.

Bring your old language into vertical alignment so that your words reflect empowerment.

When you communicate with Heart Language, life becomes infinitely creative in a flash.

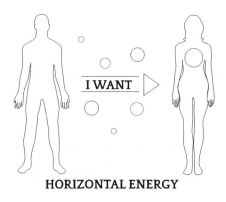

HORIZONTAL ENERGY

When you originate from need, you bring limitation into

the mix to source from others.

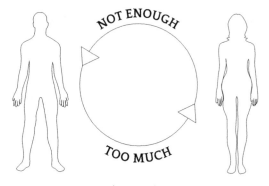

DRAMA (STORY) LOOPING

Horizontal energy and Arrowhead Language recycle and validate old stories and drama that disempower.

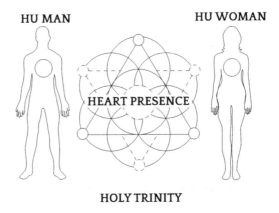

HU MAN

HU WOMAN

HEART PRESENCE

HOLY TRINITY

Humans in authentic power live beyond story to create a

field of Radical Trust with Linguistic Intelligence,

opening space for radically efficient healing

and resource manifestation.

○
○○○○
○○○○○○○
○○○○○○○○○○○
○○○○○○○○○○○○○○○
○○○○○○○○○○○○○○○○○○
○○○○○○○○○○○○○○○○○○○○○○
○○○○○○○○○○○○○○○○○○○○○○○○○○
○○○○○○○○○○○○○○○○○○○○○○○○○○○○○
○○○○○○○○○○○○○○○○○○○○○○○○○○○○○○○○○
○○○○○○○○○○○○○○○○○○○○○○○○○○○○○○○○○
○○○○○○○○○○○○○○○○○○○○○○○○○○○○○
○○○○○○○○○○○○○○○○○○○○○○○○○
○○○○○○○○○○○○○○○○○○○○○
○○○○○○○○○○○○○○○○
○○○○○○○○○○○
○○○○○○○○
○○○○
○

I AM

SOVEREIGN VERTICAL ENERGY

BE the Center of the Universe.

Use "I AM" to begin manifesting statements.

Speak with feeling, from the Heart, in present tense.

Source Father (Sky) and Momma (Earth) from Your Heart

Review

9999

Origin

See Goddess   With Heart Vision

Feel Her Essence   In Heart Presence

Honor Her Request   Intend Choiceless Choice

Listen from the Heart   Be a Center of the Universe

Open to Something New   Radically Trust Life

Own it Brothers & Sisters   We are Alchemists

Bring Desire to the Heart   For Divine Orchestration

Self Organizing Field   With Intent to Heal

Radical Guide   ***The Mirror is Your Map***

Origin

<u>The Mirror is Your Map</u>:

With self-compassion, we see the whole spectrum of life – and recognize nothing is personal and everything as a gift.

<u>New Language</u>:

I AM powerfully creating my life by bringing my language in alignment with my Heart.

○
○○○○
○○○○○○○
○○○○○○○○○○
○○○○○○○○○○○○○
○○○○○○○○○○○○○○○○
○○○○○○○○○○○○○○○○○○○
○○○○○○○○○○○○○○○○○○○○○○
○○○○○○○○○○○○○○○○○○○○○○○○○
○○○○○○○○○○○○○○○○○○○○○○○○○○○○
○○○○○○○○○○○○○○○○○○○○○○○○○○○○
○○○○○○○○○○○○○○○○○○○○○○○○○
○○○○○○○○○○○○○○○○○○○○○○
○○○○○○○○○○○○○○○○○○○
○○○○○○○○○○○○○○○○
○○○○○○○○○○○○○
○○○○○○○○○○
○○○○○○○
○○○○
○

Pain

is our power.

Challenge is our gift.

Shame comes from being told

your expression is wrong. Transcend

beyond the resistance. Allow to be in your

medicine. Surrender to being fully

alive. Expression is acceptance

of all of it. Return

to Origin.

O

Return to Origin

0000
$$0+0+0+0 = \underline{O}$$

It was known long ago that a special place was needed to help souls who had reincarnated repeatedly to work out lifetimes of collected shame and shadow so everyone could make the final ascension.

The Ascended Master's intent and design is perfectly in play.

Create a planet with hospitable climatology, clean rivers and salt water covering much of the surface as a great detoxifier.

The creation of Earth is akin to building a great amusement park perfectly designed to give people pleasure.

In the beginning, everything is shiny and new, but as the park serves it's purpose, there is wear & tear.

The purpose of the Earth is to be a playground for souls to work out their shame and shadow.

Yes, the Earth is taking wear and tear - but by design. She can handle it.

There is nothing wrong with what is happening on Earth. It is but a cycle.

Allow people to be where they are... and Radically Trust.

Yes.

Remodeling of the entire amusement park is just beginning.

Soon everything will return to shiny and new with improvements.

But It's not coming back because you humans are figuring out solutions. It's coming back because you are learning to love yourselves.

When the shame is gone and you return to love, your gratitude becomes the cleansing agent Earth requires to quickly come back into balance.

It is already happening. It is quickening and it is beyond science.

Everything is already Love. And everything is made up of exactly the same sub atomic materials.

When you simply have gratitude for all of it - Earth returns to harmony a bit more because your gratitude harmonizes every atom making up everything.

It starts with you.

You are the catalyst.

*It is **Your** love which evolves All.*

And since it's All connected, it All transforms.

Simply BE and Love everything. Love all people, starting with YOU.

Be in gratitude of each moment.

Every challenge.

And We all emerge into the highest potentiality.

All is Provided for Now.

HEART LANGUAGE

Please read this section aloud.

I learn compassion by honoring the Goddess. I learn the guidelines of the emerging consciousness of Feminine Leadership by opening my Heart to the women and men in my life, and becoming fully responsible for my healing.

Giving Her What She Wants is the mechanism.

Learning to honor the freedom of Self-expression in Her allows me to become Self-expressive in a healthy way. It shows me how to withdraw my energy from the horizontal plane, and shift my orientation to life. It allows me to become receptive.

When my energy is vertical, I recognize lustful urges as originating from scarcity. It is an expression of wanting something I perceive I do not already have. It is the expression of wanting to control, protect and covet.

When I transfer my sexual energy into my Heart I bring my desire to the Divine, and find compassion for my Self.

This orientation of surrender gives me new life experience through healing.

Honoring Her has allowed me the privilege of honoring Me. Honoring Me brings clarity to the Center of My Universe. And, like an ever-moving constellation of stars: the people, resources, events, ideas, and feelings my life requires to fully express my gift manifest perfectly in Divine timing right before my very eyes.

Life is Self-organizing around the quality of my intent and my open Heart like magic.

Thank you

HEART LANGUAGE

Please read this section aloud.

Without even realizing how, my communication becomes more compassionate. Give Her What She Wants naturally inspires me to begin utilizing the Heart Language everywhere with everyone. I feel empowered and alive.

The attractiveness of compassionate communication easefully brings new people into my life: powerful people bringing new ideas, gifts and Heart Presence.

These new people are either open to, or already speaking the Heart Language. The relationships are meaningful, richer and fuller. Time spent with people is empowering, joyful and transformative.

We are connecting from a place of instant recognition and true compassion. Our conversations are about purposeful giving, inspired action and celebrating the gift of life.

Everyone is transparently sharing their needs, dreams and inspirations - helping one another to receive exactly what they require to emerge into potential. Naturally, groups of people are forming to create and share new conscious ventures, health modalities, schools and organic gardens.

We are building new (w)holistic communities in which everyone feels at home, the children are happy, have a safe place to spend the night, and good food to eat. The community members are learning from the elders and aware of the truth coming from the mouths of children.

Creative artistic expression is highly valued and is the mechanism for our collective vision to manifest now.

All relationships are energizing to me, and I enjoy plenty of space and freedom to fully express my authentic Self. Everyone is in allowance to naturally express themselves sensually and creatively, encouraging the gift of each human expression to be amplified.

A river of energy connects us all like a web of flowing light. We are experiencing the beautiful serendipity of everything coming together and thriving harmoniously in Divine Love.

Thank you.

HEART LANGUAGE

Please read this section aloud.

My path of spiritual transformation is about alchemy. I open my Heart to the raw, darker unseen aspects of my Self and reveal them in Heart Presence. This courageous vulnerability allows the parts of me rooted in emotional love to be freed into Divine Love, initiating new openness and potentiality to emerge.

This path, while inspiring to some, unsettles others. I choose to spend my time with people who speak the Heart Language. And when it is necessary to engage people speaking the older language, I am conscious to keep my medicine digestible without alarming them, however playfully disrupting their worldview.

Thank you

○
○○○○
○○○○○○○
○○○○○○○○○○○
○○○○○○○○○○○○○○○
○○○○○○○○○○○○○○○○○○
○○○○○○○○○○○○○○○○○○○○○
○○○○○○○○○○○○○○○○○○○○○○○○
○○○○○○○○○○○○○○○○○○○○○○○○○○○
○○○○○○○○○○○○○○○○○○○○○○○○○○○○○○
○○○○○○○○○○○○○○○○○○○○○○○○○○○○○○○○
○○○○○○○○○○○○○○○○○○○○○○○○○○○○○○○
○○○○○○○○○○○○○○○○○○○○○○○○○○
○○○○○○○○○○○○○○○○○○○○○○○
○○○○○○○○○○○○○○○○○○○○
○○○○○○○○○○○○○○○○○
○○○○○○○○○○○○○○
○○○○○○○○○○○
○○○○○○○
○○○○
○

Appreciation:

Original Goddess Circle: Anya, Ava & Eliza Smith, Ashley Wilfire, Kasey Schelling, Heidi Cuppari, Martha Hartney, Prem Shakti, Rhonee Herring, Kyla Bates, Sara Ann Nelson, Nan Alpert & Tamlyn Hedemann.

Expanded Goddess Circle: Amy Lou Winstead, Ali Shanti, Kelly Moore, Lena S. A. Athena, Kate Spear, Amanda Pinelli, Brooke Andrews, Maribeth Flanagan, Stacee Harp, Elke Stokeholm, Calla Payne, Cydney Fodemen, Irina Sedova, Jana Stone, Sophia Raskin, Lily Fangz, Lindsay Mandeville, & Pippa Sorley, plus many more.

And the men... Martin, Corey, Garrett, Shamiko, Tom, Carlos, Matthew, Mighty, Brian, David, Michael, Dave, Lovejoy, Supertramp, Dustin, Travis, MysterE School Band, Robert, Timothy, Scott, Shaun, Parker, Jim, & Dan plus many more.

The Entire River House MysterE School Community.

The Eternal Evermore

○
○○○○
○○○○○○○
○○○○○○○○○○○
○○○○○○○○○○○○○○○
○○○○○○○○○○○○○○○○○○
○○○○○○○○○○○○○○○○○○○○○○
○○○○○○○○○○○○○○○○○○○○○○○○○○
○○○○○○○○○○○○○○○○○○○○○○○○○○○○○○
○○○○○○○○○○○○○○○○○○○○○○○○○○○○○○○○○○
○○○○○○○○○○○○○○○○○○○○○○○○○○○○○○○○○○
○○○○○○○○○○○○○○○○○○○○○○○○○○○○○○○○
○○○○○○○○○○○○○○○○○○○○○○○○○○○○
○○○○○○○○○○○○○○○○○○○○○○○○
○○○○○○○○○○○○○○○○○○○○
○○○○○○○○○○○○○○○
○○○○○○○○○○○
○○○○○○○
○○○○
○

Hula Appreciation:

Our Appreciation:

Her Gift to You:

Complimentary Course

www.lifeisheart.com